Contents

The Secrets of Kelp Forests

The
Secrets
of

Kelp Forests

LIFE'S EBB AND FLOW IN THE SEA'S RICHEST HABITAT

BY **HOWARD HALL**

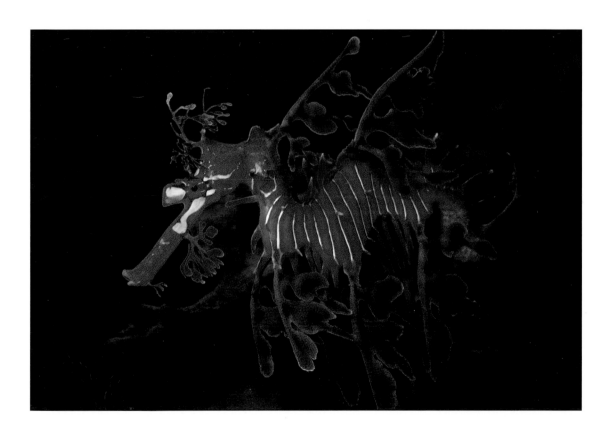

LONDON TOWN PRESS

Jean-Michel Cousteau *presents*

Publishing Director
Jean-Michel Cousteau

Series Editor
Vicki Leon

The Secrets of Kelp Forests

Principal Photographers
Howard Hall; Michele Hall

Additional Photographer
Mark Conlin

London Town Press
P.O. Box 585
Montrose, California 91021
www.LondonTownPress.com

Book design by Christy Hale
10   9   8   7   6   5   4   3   2   1
Printed in Singapore

Distributed by Publishers Group West

Library of Congress Cataloging-in-Publication Data

Hall, Howard
The secrets of kelp forests : life's ebb and flow in the sea's
richest habitat / by Howard Hall.—2nd ed.
p. cm.—(Jean-Michel Cousteau presents)
Originally published: Kelp forest. Parsippany, NJ : Silver
Burdett Press, c1995.
Includes bibliographical references and index.
ISBN 978-0-9766134-9-7 (trade paper)
1. Kelp bed ecology—Juvenile literature. 2. Kelps—Juvenile
literature. [1. Kelp bed ecology. 2. Kelps. 3. Marine animals.
4. Ecology.] I. Title.
QH541.5.K4H35 2007
577.7'8—dc22
                                        2007000298

FRONT COVER: An elephant seal, an adult bull whose nose and
chest are scarred from many battles, swims under the lush
canopy in the sea around California's Channel Islands.

TITLE PAGE: Kelp forests around the world harbor different
creatures. This amazing animal, called the leafy sea dragon,
lives in southern Australian waters. Its disguise is perfect.
The pretty "branches" on its head, muzzle, and body let it
hide in plain sight.

BACK COVER: At the shady foot of the kelp forest can be found
an ochre seastar and the pretty pink branches of gorgonian
coral. It might look like a plant, but the gorgonian is a colony
of tiny animals that feed while swaying in the ocean's surge.

TOP INSET: A blenny fish pokes its fancy headdress out of its
niche in the rocks where the kelp forest grows. Polka-dots and
frills help it hide against the patterns and colors of the reef.

MIDDLE INSET: As fearsome looking as the moray, the wolf eel
isn't an eel at all. This homely, six-foot-long blenny fish lives in
the rocky reefs of northerly forests where bull kelp predominates.
For dinner, it goes after lobster and urchins. BOTTOM INSET:
The graceful bulbs of the kelp plant are hollow but they're not
empty. These glowing golden floats are filled with gases that
hold up the heavy plants.

A great golden wilderness

◀ Dancing to the rhythm of the sea, great stands of kelp sway in the surge, lit by a golden sun shining through Pacific waters.

I was a 17-year-old kid the first time I entered the most mysterious and magical place on our planet. I had no idea what to expect.

In water so clear I could see nearly 100 feet in all directions, I dived down into the sea. My body felt as though it had wings. I flew among giant "trees" in an underwater cathedral. Long lemon fronds of kelp swayed overhead, dancing to the rhythm of the ocean's surge. No birds sang here. No flowers bloomed. There was no trace of human activity. I had entered the amber wilderness of the kelp forest.

As I neared the ocean floor, an orange garibaldi fish popped out of a lime-green thicket of eel grasses to make friends. A few minutes later, a curious sea lion did a loop-the-loop in my direction to blow bubbles at me.

In places, the leafy canopy over my head was so thick that the sunlight vanished. When a giant seabass appeared, it looked like a fishy monster with a huge rubber-lipped mouth. My adrenalin was pumping. I was only a few miles from my California home, but this felt like another, more enchanted world.

◄ A garibaldi youngster stares at the camera. This often curious, sometimes aggressive fish is even prettier as a juvenile, wearing its electric blue polka-dots.

▼ As it works its way under drift kelp, the mola mola sunfish gets fishy company. The mola mola's odd shape and its cartoon eyes and mouth make it a favorite of underwater photographers.

Jim Nerison, my diving buddy, signaled me to swim toward another stand of kelp. We found ourselves at the edge of a cliff, looking down at a sandy plain, 40 feet below. Dozens of bat rays flew over the plain, their deltoid wings rippling in unison, graceful as ballet dancers. From time to time, they touched the sand, searching for crustaceans to eat. Whenever the bat rays touched down, angel sharks, some as big as five feet across, exploded from the sand, hurrying away to find another spot to conceal themselves.

I'll never forget the golden twilight of that underwater jungle, its shadows as deep as my imagination. Those undersea cliffs at its edge, the fearless curiosity of the animals, the angel sharks bursting from their hiding places, the bat rays soaring over the white sandy plain. It remains one of my most wonderful experiences underwater.

The day those memories were made happened long ago. The world's kelp forests are still the most beautiful wilderness I've ever seen. It's a sad fact, however, that as the world's human population has grown, kelp forests and their once-teeming populations of fishes, sea otters, and angel sharks have dwindled.

As a youngster, I used to think that the kelp forests off the southern California coast and around the Channel Islands were the only places they occurred. Gradually I learned that these ecosystems are found in many coastal areas. Over the years, I've been lucky enough to dive them off southern Australia and New Zealand; near South Africa; along the north Atlantic coast of Canada; and in places off the Pacific and Atlantic coasts of South America. Kelp forests also occur off northeast Asia, around sub-Antarctic islands and Antarctica itself. They tend to be most plentiful in the Pacific waters from Alaska to Baja California.

What do kelp forests need to thrive? A certain amount of wave action, creating a place where lively seawater mixes with lots of nutrients. Clear cool seawater between 40 and 72 degrees Fahrenheit. And hard surfaces to cling to, like granite reefs. Instead of tree roots, kelp attaches itself to rocks with a tangled mass of finger-like fibers called a holdfast. The fibers, called *haptera*, interwine and glue the base of the plant to rock. This super-glue is one of mother nature's strongest adhesives.

Kelp, especially *Macrocystis*, the giant species, has generous amounts of what biologists call "leaf index." One giant kelp

▲ Giant kelp plants have no roots. Instead they attach to rocky reefs with holdfasts. Each holdfast puts out many finger-like projections.

"tree" provides about 14 square feet of living space for each square foot it covers on the seafloor. Plant for plant, the kelp ecosystem, along with coral reefs and rainforests, rank as the most biodiverse habitats on the planet.

How long have these rich ecosystems been around? Scientists have discovered that there once was a nearly continuous chain of kelp forests from Japan to Alaska and down the Pacific coast into South America. As early as 20,000 years ago, these forests may have served as a "kelp highway" for adventurous human beings traveling by boat from Asia to the New World. Kelp forests would have provided access to crabs, fishes, and other edibles. The sturdy stands of kelp offshore would have reduced wave action, making it easier for the canoes of early voyagers to navigate the Pacific.

Until 1943 and the invention of the self-contained underwater breathing apparatus we now call scuba, few human beings had ever entered the kelp forest habitat. Once divers began to slip beneath the ocean's surface, however, they found a place as crowded with life as any tropical rainforest, located only a stone's throw away from cities, highways, and human activity.

Even now, when the world's oceans are visited by millions of divers and countless underwater photographers like me, surprisingly few people know how magical—and useful—a kelp forest is. To kids and grownups living along North American coasts, "kelp" is that sometimes-stinky heap of seaweed washed up on the beach. Fishermen and boaters often think of kelp as a nuisance,

▼ This bug-eyed bulldog of a fish has a name to match its appearance. Called the sarcastic fringehead, it lives in crevices, sandy holes, and sometimes in bottles thrown away by human beings.

▶A foot-long garibaldi fish lights up a California kelp forest with its orangy-red body. Male garibaldis defend their territories fiercely. Their flashy colors may serve to warn off male rivals.

▼ Giant kelp can be 100 feet tall. A plant that size weighs a lot. To reach the sunlight it needs, the kelp grows round, gas-filled floats on the ends of its blades and fronds.

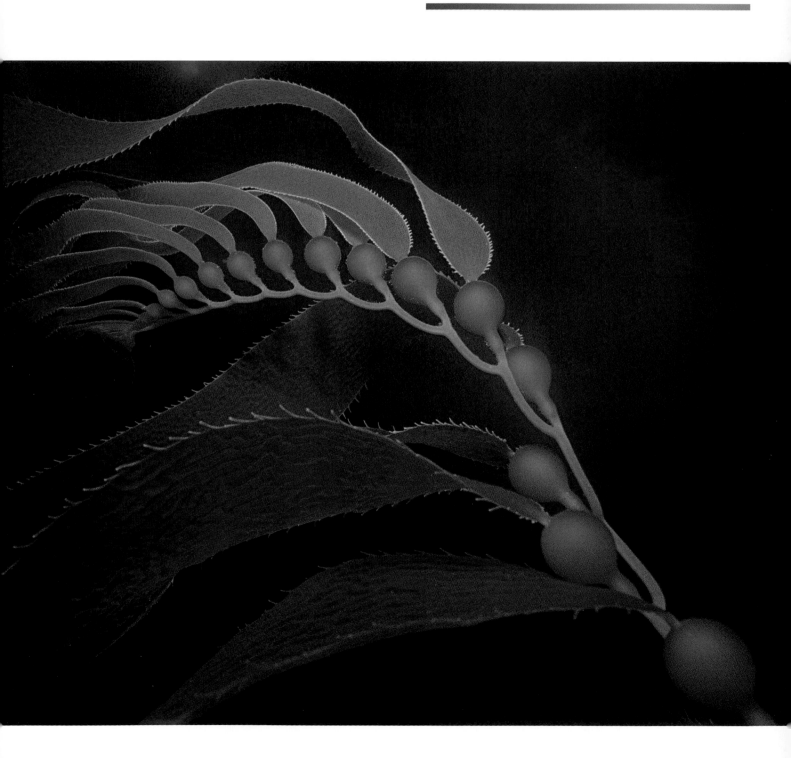

a tangled mass that can foul boat propellers.

The true nature of this wonderful plant can only be seen beyond the surfline, where stands of living kelp flourish. There, in and on and around each plant live millions of residents, small and large. At times tiny hydroids and bryozoan moss animals cover the kelp blades with thousands of their flowery bodies. To fishes and animals without backbones, these undersea forests serve as hiding places, nurseries for their young, and hunting grounds. To seals, whales, sharks, and other large animals, the kelp forest is a supermarket they visit often. To sea otters, the kelp forest provides food, a playpen for their pups, and a nightly bed. In an economic sense as well as an ecological one, the value of kelp forests rivals that of any forest found on land.

The "timber" of this forest, however, is kelp. Large aquatic plants are divided into three main groups or *phyla* of algae: red, green, or brown. Kelp belongs to the brown algae group. More than 20 species populate the cool Pacific waters off North America. The largest? *Macrocystis pyrifera*, known as giant kelp, and the world's biggest aquatic plant. Growing in waters as deep as 130 feet, Macrocystis reaches all the way to the surface. Giant kelp dominates the forests it grows in; in colder waters, though, the bull kelp (*Nereocystis luetkeana*) rules. This kelp looks more like a palm tree, with a single long stipe and bushy blades at its bulbous top. Smaller species grow in the shade of the big guys, including understory kelp and feather-boa kelp.

A kelp's great height doesn't depend on a thick wooden trunk. Instead, it has extra-long, flexible stalks or stems, called stipes. Instead of branches, each kelp plant has fronds—sometimes hundreds of them. In place of leaves, it has wide blades. Some kelp species grow round or pear-shaped floats, called *pneumatocysts*, at the base of their blades. These gas-filled floats act like balloons, keeping the heavy fronds, loaded with countless animal hitchhikers, from sinking. Floats allow the plant to zoom toward the surface. And sunlight.

Like plants on land, kelp requires sunlight to live. Primarily through its broad blades, it converts solar energy and carbon dioxide into food through the process called photosynthesis. Sunlight supplies the energy. The kelp pulls nourishment from nutrient-rich seawater, which supplies nitrates, carbon dioxide and other needs.

A giant kelp may live six years or more; like the leaves on a tree, its blades and fronds grow, die off, and fall to the forest floor.

When mature, *Macrocystis* can measure 200 feet from its holdfast to the tips of its fronds. Giant kelp is speedy as well as big. It competes with bamboo for the title of world's fastest-growing plant.

If I had a practical way to stay underwater all day, I could literally watch kelp grow! Near the surface where sunlight is plentiful, kelp may shoot up as much as two feet per day. Once the blades and fronds reach the surface, they don't stop; instead, they spread and intertwine with other kelp plants to form a floating, dancing canopy over the forest.

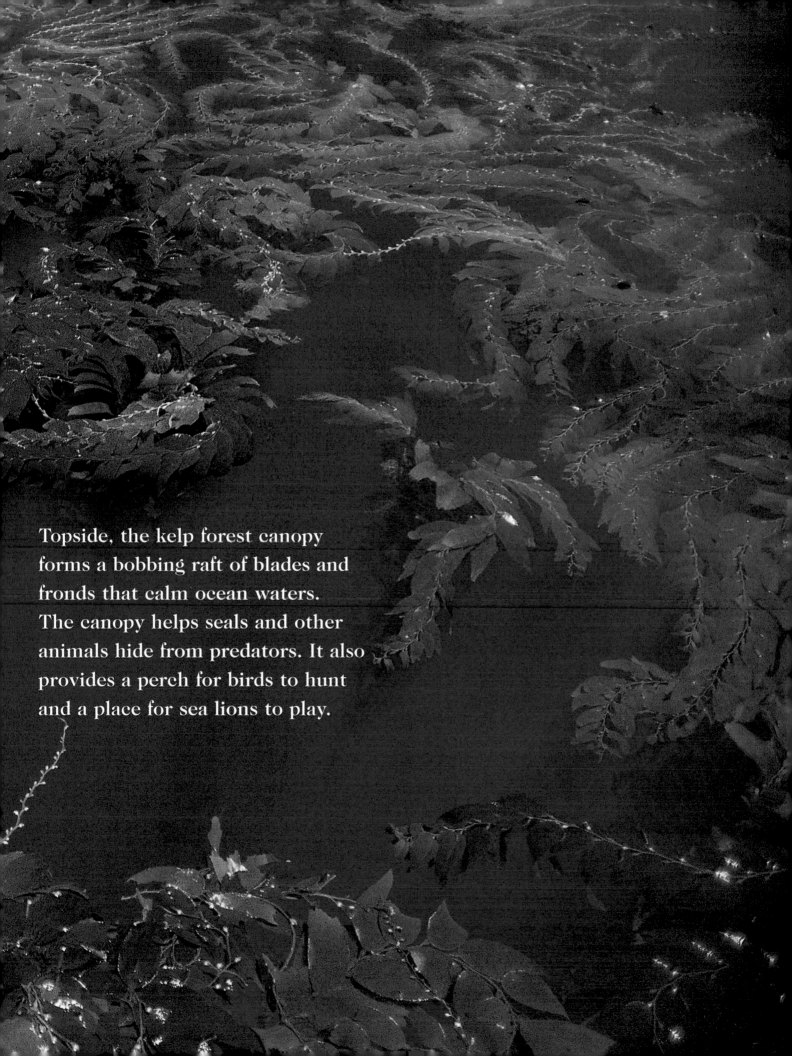

Topside, the kelp forest canopy forms a bobbing raft of blades and fronds that calm ocean waters. The canopy helps seals and other animals hide from predators. It also provides a perch for birds to hunt and a place for sea lions to play.

*I*f you look at the surface of the sea from above, the canopy resembles a bruise-colored mass on the water. Even up close, the golden-brown blades and bobbing bulbs of the kelp forest canopy give little hint of the beauty beneath. Or the activity. Just below the surface, hundreds of species play hide and seek.

As the sun sends long shafts of light through the amber-colored fronds, small fishes and juveniles of larger species graze, keeping an eye out for predators like the

◄ Schooling fish, such as jack mackerel, often move in and out of the kelp forest. Why do fish school? Greater safety in numbers, for one thing. Swirling schools also tend to confuse predators. Schooling together assures that almost every jack mackerel will meet a mate and reproduce.

◄Harbor seals and other pinnipeds sometimes use the kelp forest to hunt for fishes or squid. This habitat lets them hide out from serious enemies, like sharks. The thick tangle of the canopy makes a safe, gently rocking bed for seal naps. It's also a bouncy place to sun-bask and play pinniped games.

►Sea otters are regular shoppers in the kelp forest. Females anchor pups to kelp while they hunt for groceries. To propel herself, this female uses her strong webbed hind feet. Her sensitive front paws can find clams even in the dark.

kelp bass. Many species wear colors and markings to match the plants they live among; the giant kelpfish even imitates the swaying movements of its plant home. Various species of crabs and mollusks climb the stipes and clamber over fronds, feeding on colonies of smaller animals. Heights work well for them. The upper story offers safer quarters from hungry seastars at the foot of the kelp.

A variety of turban snails and top snails have a kelp forest address. The Norris's top snail spends much of its time climbing. Once this stout mollusk with the orangy-red shell reaches the top of a giant kelp, it lets go and plummets to the bottom, where it seeks out another plant and starts another rise-and-fall cycle. While in the canopy, it crunches kelp while trying to avoid seagulls,

a bird well known for its taste for escargot.

Other birds besides gulls frequent the canopy. Murrelets, herons, egrets, and terns find its bouncy trampoline of tangled vegetation a dandy place to fish and feed. From this platform, they stalk small fry like kelp clingfish and juvenile rockfishes. Not far below the canopy, schools of adult rockfish circle, feeding on microscopic plankton.

Many animals make kelp their main meal. Opaleyes, halfmoon perches, sheephead, and other fishes eat *Macrocystis* and other kelp. So do smaller vegetarians like the shrimplike isopods.

Larger animals from elephant seals to sea lions find the canopy a refuge. Harbor seals rest on the buoyant surface, safely concealed from sharks by thick fronds.

At night, they travel to open waters, diving up to 400 feet for fish and squid.

Sea lions also hunt at night, spending their days basking or playing in the kelp. They love to show off—and few other marine mammals have their speed or grace. If white sharks could be surveyed, nine out of ten would pick sea lions as their menu favorite. They have little chance, however, of catching an alert animal. Sea lions even heckle sharks. The sleek, doglike pinnipeds seem to enjoy testing their courage by diving down and nipping at the tail or dorsal fin of the great white. The shark doesn't appear to mind—it just keeps patrolling around the perimeter of the kelp forest.

Days may go by. Eventually a sea lion gets careless, forgetting there is a single-minded shark about. Perhaps the sea lion decides to nap. Or it gets busy, barking at other pinnipeds on shore. It only takes one unguarded minute. In a flash, the apparently uninterested shark switches directions, rushing upward and taking the sea lion in a blaze of power and teeth.

Sea otters rely on the kelp canopy even more than the pinnipeds. When they need to dive to hunt, female otters tie a kelp frond around their pups. Mom and pup also snooze, nurse, and sun themselves in the canopy, later wrapping up like burritos in the kelp to rest in nature's "water bed" for the night. In daylight hours, adult otters snorkel through the canopy, chugging along as they strip fronds of crabs, snails, urchins, and other easy-to-reach goodies.

Mystery creatures of the understory & rocky reef

Kelp plants continuously produce new fronds and blades that grow toward the surface. Like leaves in a hardwood forest, they break off, drift away, or sink slowly to the seafloor. This process, called sloughing, makes room for new growth.

Dead plant matter doesn't last long. Some animals, like the kelp crab, use drift kelp as shell décor to hide from predators. But for many fishes and invertebrates, drift kelp is breakfast, lunch, and dinner.

◀ An alien from outer space? No, it's a mantis shrimp. To terrify prey, this bizarre crustacean rears up to show off its weapons. Those claws can break through aquarium glass! This misnamed fellow isn't a shrimp or a praying mantis. It's a fierce hunter whose eyes see in color and in several directions at once.

▲ When alarmed, plumose anemones in sherbet colors may close up into tight barrels. Others stay open for the business of eating. Their flowery "heads" are tentacles that grab and sting.

Abalone, for example. A large mollusk, the ab grips the rocky reef with a powerful muscle called a foot. A single sturdy shell armors the animal, protecting it from predators. Like other mollusks, it can protrude a slippery "skin" or mantle over its shell, usually keeping seastars and other attackers from getting a grip. The ab spends most of its life attached to the same rock, waiting for home delivery of its drift kelp.

Kelp stands attach themselves to rocky reefs, which are often encrusted with deep layers of anemones, sponges, sea squirts, and other marine species. The brilliance, variety, and color of this display astonishes me every time I see it. Pigments inside the tissues of certain nudibranchs, algae, and

▼ Flowery anemones, bat stars, barnacles, and other filter feeders wait for ocean currents to deliver dinner. What do they eat? Bits of drift kelp and a "soup" of tiny floating animals called plankton. Bigger anemones can also kill larger prey, such as crabs and fishes, with their stinging tentacles.

anemones are able to fluoresce into spectacular reds and oranges. Whenever I swim over the rocky reef, they glow like a treasure chest of precious stones under a blacklight.

Most of this encrusting life looks plantlike. You could easily mistake an anemone for a flower blossom; a gorgonian coral for a bush; or a finger sponge for a succulent plant. Surprise: most are stay-at-home animals. Although not quick or dangerous, these often-hungry beauties are meat-eaters. Anemones and gorgonian corals, for instance, wait for plankton and other small prey to drift near. Their tentacles, armed with stinging cells called nematocysts, harpoon the prey. Larger anemones tackle even bigger victims, from fishes to crabs.

The kelp forest floor and its reef rocks are studded with hidey-holes, caves, and canyons. These provide homes for hunters

▶ Its burning bush beauty resembles a feathery land plant but the gorgonian coral is an animal—and a hungry one. Each slender stalk contains thousands of tiny polyps. They wait for even smaller animals to float within snapping distance. INSET: Like its anemone cousins, the gorgonian coral is armed with nematocysts. These weapons look and act like miniature harpoons, delivering poison to their victim.

and hunted. Both predators and prey often use cryptic coloration as a strategy, wearing colors and patterns to blend in. Many sport dazzling wardrobes and textures that match the sizzling colors of their surroundings.

The foot-long spotted scorpionfish, for example, resembles nearby rocks, becoming almost invisible to a diver a few feet away. When a tiny fish ventures near, the scorpionfish reacts with split-second speed, sucking the fish into its mouth and swallowing it whole.

Many other bottom-dwelling fishes, from turbots and rockfishes to blennies and sculpins, use camouflage to hunt—and to avoid being dinner for others. Invertebrates adopt the same tactics. With their nimble claws, decorator crabs plant anemones,

▼ A sea hare releases a purple "smoke screen" to confuse predators. This member of the sea slug family wears stripes and spots to blend into its busy background of rocks and algae.

colorful sponges, and algae on their backs and legs. Until they move, they are almost impossible to spot.

The Grand Master of camouflage? The octopus. This talented cephalopod takes on the texture, shape, and color of its surroundings, from sand to wildly colored coralline algae. One minute you see a bright red octopus sitting on the kelp forest floor. The next, it's gone—or so it seems. Its skin, loaded with pigment cells called chromatophores, make the octopus the marine Houdini.

When not stalking prey, the soft-skinned octopus uses camouflage to keep from becoming lunch for seals, large fishes, and its greatest enemy, the moray eel. Although the eel has poor eyesight, its sense of smell is second to none. When a moray

▼ An octopus pauses to adjust its color and texture to match the pink coralline algae and rocks it glides across. A very smart mollusk, it has special skin cells that let it quick-change. It can even vanish in a cloud of inky smoke.

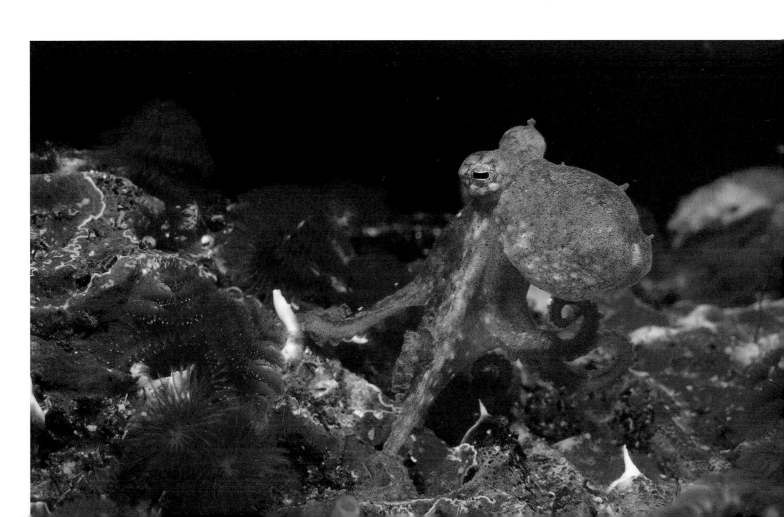

gets a whiff of octopus, it attacks. The octopus shoots a defensive ink cloud that works two ways. First it lets the octopus "vanish" like a magician; second, this smoke-screen contains an anesthetic that temporarily deadens the eel's sense of smell. If the octopus manages to escape by leaving behind one or more of its arms, the eel can't smell the animal well enough to pursue. The eel must content itself with an octopus-arm snack. And the octopus? In a fairly short time it can regrow its lost limbs, a process called autotomy.

Although kelp forest creatures are clever at disguises, some residents call attention to themselves with bold colors. The Catalina goby shimmers with neon-bright oranges and blues. And the garibaldi fish, fiery as a Hawaiian sunset, seems to have no worries at all. Neither humans nor fishy predators find it very tasty—and it's a legally protected species.

◄ Which kelp forest resident has a face only a mother could love? The moray eel. It lurks in rocky holes, able to wiggle through tight spots, thanks to its mucus-coated skin. A night hunter, it strikes at octopus and fish with razor-blade teeth and jaws of iron. Because it has no gills, it must open its mouth constantly to breathe. The moray might look scary but it's timid.

▼ Underwater photographers know from experience how garibaldi fishes feel about urchins. When male garibaldis prepare nests for their young, they often haul away urchin intruders like this big red one from their nesting sites.

Garibaldi fish make their nests on rocky reefs within the kelp forest. That is, the male does. First he chooses a suitable nesting site on the side of a rock, then spends days removing all growth from it except for several species of small red algae. These he prunes and cultivates into a lush circular patch about 18 inches across. As proud of his spread as a suburban husband is of his

◄ Hooded nudibranchs cling by the hundreds to kelp blades and eel grass. Like transparent fisher folk, they move their see-through nets to and fro to catch bits of plankton drifting by.

▲ The hairy hermit crab, a busy fellow, may reach four inches long on its diet of drift kelp and dead matter. As it grows, its borrowed shell gets too small. To solve the housing problem, it often steals a bigger shell from another hermit crab.

lawn, the garibaldi male sets out to show the female of his species the job he's done. Swimming several feet above the nest, he clucks three times whenever a prospective mate passes near, hoping she will follow him. When his nest succeeds in impressing a female, she lays her eggs in the algae patch— then swims off, leaving the rest to the male.

He, on the other hand, sometimes keeps on looking and may attract more than one female to his nest. After fertilizing all the eggs, he looks after them for two weeks, cleaning and protecting his offspring from would-be predators. Once the babies hatch, however, the garibaldi new dad takes little notice. As they drift off, he continues to guard the empty nest.

Unlike most babies in the animal world, young garibaldi are even more stunning than their citrus-bright parents. The juveniles have luscious orange bodies dotted with electric blue spots.

The rocky reef, and the kelp stands growing from it, are crawling with other colorful characters. Some of the smallest yet most dazzling are members of the nudibranch family, dressed in patterns, shapes, and colors jazzier than the gaudiest fishing lure. These soft, helpless-looking animals are marine slugs or snails without shells.

The colors they wear might seem to announce: "I'm delicious. Snack on me!"

But predators have learned they mean: "Snack on me and you'll be sorry!" Most nudibranchs have a vile taste; some are poisonous. Still others taste bad and sting, too! A few nudibranchs lack a wild wardrobe. One is the hooded nudibranch, a see-through beauty that carries a filmy "net" to trap plankton. It attaches itself to kelp blades and is often found there in huge numbers.

A crowd of organisms also live in, on, and under the holdfast of each kelp. Between the pink, red, and blue fingers of the haptera hide shrimp, brittle stars, worms, copepods, and juvenile abalone. Mussels, clams, brooding anemones, and swell sharks also crowd in, while hermit crabs and nudibranchs roam. As many as 180 species have been counted on a single holdfast.

Life & death in kelp forest clearings

▶At times the kelp forest gets unusual visitors. A deep-sea jellyfish, such as this rare specimen, is brought by ocean currents. Even though the jellyfish has super-toxic tentacles, the fearless garibaldi fish finds it good eating.

Like forests on land, kelp forests have sandy clearings here and there. In the sea, the sandy plain at the outer edge of a kelp forest may be at the bottom of a steep slope or a reef's edge. The first time I saw it, the sandy plain appeared lifeless. But I learned to watch patiently, waiting for its secretive citizens to reveal themselves.

Halibut, angel sharks, turbot, and flounder bury themselves up to their eyes. When a meal possibility swims near, they strike upwards, swift and deadly as a lightning bolt.

Other animals like the red octopus burrow in sand to hide from predators.

It huddles there or in worm holes, emerging at night to forage for food. Other timid night feeders, from heart urchins to cusk eels, also remain buried during the day.

Being buried in sand doesn't offer complete protection from being eaten, however. Many rays and sharks have sense organs that tune into the weak electrical fields of other animals. Horn sharks, stingrays, and thornback rays all cruise the sandy bottom in this manner, honing in on invisible prey.

The kelp forest and its sandy plains go through what we might call seasons on land. In spring, kelp plants experience

▶ The lizardfish dozes under the sand, keeping one eye periscoped for danger. Sharks are one. With special sensing organs, sharks roam the sandy plain like metal detectors, spotting even a well-buried lizardfish.

new growth, and by mid-summer are at their thickest. As fall and winter arrive, the fronds and blades become ragged, many falling off as drift kelp.

Kelp animal species also have cycles of birth, growth, and dormancy as land-based species do, giving this ecosystem a different look as the year turns.

In early spring the sandy plain, sometimes lying 100 feet below the surface, gets as crowded as a big-city intersection. Millions

▶ Predators like rays and whales attend an all-you-can-eat banquet of dead and dying squid. So do smaller fishes and scavengers. With so much food, the eaters soon get full. They pay no attention to the mounds of eggs. In a few weeks, the eggs hatch and a new generation of squid is born.

▼ Each spring, huge numbers of squid swim from the ocean depths to meet, mate, and die near the kelp forest. Before dying, the females lay millions of eggs, which soon cover the sandy plain with snowy drifts in all directions.

of deep-water squid rise from the depths to spawn in the sand at the forest's edge. Enormous schools of male and female squid meet and mate almost simultaneously. It's a startling spectacle, the water filled with zigzagging animals on the chase, their sleek bodies iridescent with excitement.

After mating, the female produces an egg-case nearly half the length of her body. Carrying it, she digs deep into the sand,

▲ Spiny lobsters scuttle and swim backwards to get around. Their main enemies? Wolf eels. They attack when lobsters have molted their shells and wear no armor. Large lobsters, once common in California kelp forests, are now as rare as diamonds.

anchoring the egg-case. Soon millions upon millions of egg cases turn the sandy plain into an alien garden. Latecomers are forced to anchor their cases to clusters of other eggs—that's how crowded things get. Eventually, a soft white blanket of squid egg cases, sometimes two feet thick, extends over many acres of sand next to the kelp forest.

After spawning, all of the adult squid die. The first time I saw it, I couldn't believe my eyes. They died by the millions! Perhaps for this reason the squid pay no attention to predators during their mating and egg-laying. For the squid, time is short and they focus on reproduction. Being eaten? A minor concern.

Many marine animals dine on squid. For them, spawning time is an all-you-can-eat restaurant, open 24/7. Sea lions and harbor seals, sharks and bat rays, lobsters and crabs, dolphins and whales all gather to feast on the easy pickings. Try as they might, even the hungriest predators can't consume all the squid.

After they get their fill, thousands of dead bodies still litter the sandy plain among the egg cases. Now it's the turn of smaller predators and scavengers to stuff themselves.

Predators and scavengers big and small ignore the squid eggs. Either they don't taste good, or the diners are so full of squid meat that they have no appetite left. Whatever the reason, the squid eggs are left to hatch.

Each egg case contains about 200 eggs. In two weeks or so, the eggs mature, the baby squid hatching to drift away as part of the living soup of the sea called plankton. Where these young squid go and what they do during the next two years is virtually unknown. In their third year, however, they usually return to the same clearing to spawn like their parents and begin the cycle anew.

In early summer, long after the newborn squid have vanished into the open ocean, bat rays begin to gather along the outer edge of the forest. In the evening, these beautiful bird-like creatures, some with wingspans of five feet or more, form vast swirling schools. I've often watched and filmed as the great diamond shapes of the bat rays circle above me, looking like a column of rising air beneath a thundercloud. Thousands of rays eventually join the party.

As the evening turns into night, the bat rays court. The male swims beneath the female, caressing her stomach with his back. Often she rejects him, darting away with rapid beats of her wings. If he finally wins her approval, they mate. The morning after, the rays settle into the sand, wingtip touching wingtip as far as the eye can see. All day they rest, waiting for the sun to set so they may begin once again their long and tender courtship patterns.

On the sandy clearings, strange and bitter battles also take place. One of the most bizarre is that of the rainbow nudibranch. This shocking-pink sea slug gyrates through the water like a hip-hop dancer. To this feisty hunter, nothing sounds yummier than biting off the toxic tentacles of a tube anemone. Most creatures under the sea avoid eating corals, hydroids, and anemones because they carry those poisonous weapons, nematocysts.

▼ Blood star is a good name for these smooth-skinned orange or bright red seastars. Are they on tip-toe? No, they are spawning. Eggs and sperm fall from holes between their arms. In this species, the female carries fertilized eggs around with her until the young hatch out.

Huge swirling groups of bat rays
meet and mate in the kelp forest
clearings. These beautiful animals,
some with wingspans of five feet or
more, gather in summer for their
courtships in slow motion.

▶ Once the rainbow gobbles down some of the anemone's tentacles, it transfers the unfired harpoons to its own feathery gills. Now they will protect the nudibranch. Afterward, the rainbow lays a lacy white string of eggs on top of the anemone. When the anemone's tentacles grow back, they will also protect the nudibranch's tasty eggs from predators.

▲ Like other sea slugs, rainbow nudibranchs thrive on deadly foods. These shocking pink animals attack tall tube anemones, going for the waving tentacles, chock-full of tiny harpoons filled with poison.

Not the rainbow nudibranch. It makes a career of crawling from one tube anemone to the next, inching up the tube, and lunging at the tentacles. This strange slug doesn't even bother to lunch on the rest of the anemone—only the poisonous part! The rest of this eat-and-be-eaten scenario is equally amazing. The nudibranch eats all or most of the tentacles—but does not digest them. Instead, it's able to move the stinging cells through its body to the fluffy gills along its back. The transplanted harpoons remain alive and armed, protecting the nudibranch from any animal foolish enough to tackle this small but incredibly hardy hunter.

The rainbow nudibranch isn't unique. Many sea slugs dine on anemones and on colonies of small animals called hydroids, borrowing their venom-filled weapons in the same way. Sea slugs are tough as tigers and let predators know it by wearing some of the boldest colors and most fantastic body ornaments under the sea.

Above the sandy plains and around the kelp forest edges, much bigger predators than the rainbow nudibranch tend to gather. Because the vegetation of the kelp forest is so thick, most prey can easily outmaneuver big predators. For that reason, blue sharks and makos hang out along the edges, waiting for fishy inhabitants to venture out a little too far.

Saving our kelp forests

◀ A ray meets its death in a gill net. Fishermen regularly use drift nets, purse seine nets, and gill nets to fish. Such huge nets, however, capture everything underwater for miles. A sickening number of sea creatures are caught and thrown away as useless, called by-catch or incidental kill.

You may be surprised at the big influence weather has on the environment under the sea. Storms produce strong winds that blow across the ocean surface, creating waves. Underwater, the waves passing overhead are felt as surge. The larger the wave, the stronger the surge and the deeper it penetrates.

As an underwater filmmaker, I've had way too much personal experience with this savage power. Strong surge feels like a hurricane blowing one direction for 30 seconds, then in the opposite direction for another half minute. In powerful surge, a diver may be tumbled across the ocean floor like a trashcan in a tornado. It's far worse when you are hanging onto camera gear for dear life—like the 150-pound IMAX® camera I often drag.

These storms can devastate the forest, tearing kelp holdfasts from the rocky reef. At times, entire forests are ripped loose. A monster storm will destroy nearly every stand of kelp forest for hundreds of miles along the coast. But when the sun comes out again, new kelp plants soon begin

▶ The pink-and-black sheephead fish has buck teeth, giving it a risk-free way to nibble prickly food like sea urchins. This fish and the sea otter are the kelp forest's main allies. They keep urchin populations from chewing down the plants. As the populations of sheephead and sea otters get more endangered, urchin numbers expand, bulldozing more kelp forests.

▲ Sea urchins normally live in urchin-sized holes they chew out of rocks. But when predators like sea otters are not there to keep their numbers down, urchins become a plague. Their populations skyrocket, jamming up to 300 urchins into one square yard. INSET: When urchins get out of control, they move through the kelp forest, chewing up every plant in their path. They even eat the holdfasts of the kelp. What's left of the forest floats away, to wash up on the beach.

germinating on the reef. If conditions are good, fast-growing forests will return to their former lushness in less than a year.

A much more serious threat to *Macrocystis* forests is a rise in seawater temperatures caused by El Nino events. This two to seven-year cycle brings warm-water currents close to the Pacific Coast where normally there would be cooler water. El Nino events are natural—but are getting stronger and more frequent. Between 1980 and 2006, the world saw a huge increase in their intensity and frequency. During El Nino events, kelp forests may die off on a global scale and take many years to recover. It doesn't take much heat to murder a kelp forest. All it takes is seawater that gets warmer by a few degrees.

The worst threat of all, however, not just to kelp forests but to our entire planet, is global warming. Thousands of scientific studies show that global warming, sometimes called the greenhouse effect, is largely due to human activity. Most of it comes from burning fossil fuels, which puts more carbon dioxide into the air.

By increasing the chances of more extreme weather and El Nino events, global warming has the power to wipe out whole marine ecosystems, from kelp forests to coral reefs.

That's not the last of the bad news, either. The kelp forest has an animal enemy: the sea urchin, particularly the purple species.

▲ Using their tube feet, bat stars flip sea urchins over to get at the unprotected parts. Here, two bat stars squabble over dinner. To get inside the urchin's shell, the hungry hunters will project their stomachs clear outside their leathery bodies.

These nonstop plant chompers have an insatiable appetite for kelp.

Before human beings exploited fishery resources off California and the rest of the Pacific Coast in a big way, nature maintained a balance that kept the kelp forest healthy. Kelp-eating urchins were kept in check by sea otters and sheephead fish. Today, however, sea otters are highly endangered in their northern California range and no longer found off southern California at all. The sheephead has been heavily overfished, reducing its influence to almost nothing.

Without enough predators to keep their numbers stable, urchin populations explode. Like army ants in slow motion, they move by the millions through the ecosystem, devouring all the kelp in their path.

Worse yet, they eat the tough holdfasts too, setting the kelp forest adrift. Afterward, only barren rock remains. It's a horrifying sight—one I've seen way too often in my 30 years of diving.

Gill-netting is another disaster for kelp forest animals. Commercial fishermen circle the kelp forest and enter it, using gill nets to catch white seabass, halibut, soupfin sharks, and angel sharks. But these huge nets capture many other creatures, which fishermen throw back, dead or dying, into the water. The fishing industry calls it "by-catch" or "incidental kill." Very often, the amount of incidental kill is much bigger than the harvest of marketable fish.

Diving where gill nets have been used is a heartbreaking experience. One year during the bat-ray mating season, I swam out to a sandy plain near the kelp forest.

The ocean floor with littered with hundreds of bat rays—caught and killed thoughtlessly, then discarded as useless.

A fishery that wastes so many valuable animals is very disturbing to me. You probably feel the same way. The blame can't be put entirely on commercial fishermen, however. In today's world, the fisherman tries to make a living under almost impossible conditions. There is more public demand for seafood worldwide. There is more competition from fishermen from many nations, some with goals of getting the catch at any cost. And there are fewer fish to be caught. Always fewer fish.

The nearshore environment of the kelp forest isn't immune to pollution, either. As long ago as 1950, studies off California showed that industrial waste and human sewage going into the ocean made the water murkier. The lack of light stunted kelp growth and the kelp beds shrank alarmingly.

Given these huge, horrendous problems, are there any solutions?

The first step is to make the general public much more aware of the value of the kelp forest. Seafood forms a big part of the American diet and it's in everyone's best interest to keep the kelp forests healthy. Vast amounts of fish and shellfish still come from the kelp forest; but as a nursery for the young of many species, it has even more value.

This forest also produces a sustainable, valuable crop that doesn't have scales or claws. It's kelp itself. The cell walls of the big kelps contain a super-useful compound called algin. It's used to make everything from toothpaste to ice cream, from textiles to canned goods. When used in preparations

▲ A blue shark loses its life in a gill net, just one of the manmade hazards in its ocean home. Fishing gear strangles sharks and seals. Plastic loops become deathtraps for birds, whales, and baby pinnipeds. Keeping the kelp forest—and the sea—free of human junk is a big step toward saving our planet.

like salad dressing, algin keeps liquids from separating and makes them thicker and smoother. Besides eating it daily and wearing it, all of us use many products containing algin, from cosmetics to car tires, from paints to paper.

Once thought useful only to make potash or fertilizer, kelp is now commercially harvested off California, Washington, Mexico, Norway, Scotland, Newfoundland, China, Chile, Tasmania, France, and Spain.

Since kelp is fast-growing, the top of the canopy is "mowed" to a depth of three to four feet. Large vessels pass over the kelp, cutting and gathering it. In California alone, kelp beds are licensed or leased to harvesters, producing 200,000 tons or more of kelp a year.

Kelp is also harvested for use as "baby food" to feed tiny abalones, grown on aquaculture farms in California and elsewhere. Another growing market for edible kelp exists in Asia, where people have a long tradition of including kelp in their diets.

In the 21st century, kelp forests have become a travel destination for divers and sports fishermen. They look on kelp forests as a marine paradise, as primary habitat for lobsters, abalone, rock scallops, and certain fish species. They look on the kelp forest as a resource to be protected.

The biggest fans of the kelp forest are scuba divers and snorkelers, especially those like me who hunt with cameras instead of spearguns.

Compared to the land, where countless habitats and places of natural beauty have been degraded, polluted, or chopped to pieces by human development, the kelp forest remains essentially untamed. Even in the forests frequented by divers, you won't find a human footprint. Or a trail that must be followed. Or a park ranger directing traffic.

Those of us who dive these kelp forests are lucky beyond belief. We get to wander through a vast wilderness, a place of adventure and solitude, nearby yet invisible to our workaday world. The kelp forest remains a true wilderness habitat. It's not immune to pressures exerted from our growing human populations, however. It's not protected from pollution or destruction by uncaring people, either.

From outer space our planet is blue; it is ocean. What we discard into the sea does not vanish. What we do to its creatures comes back to haunt us. Poisoning our atmosphere affects the weather under the sea as surely as the air we breathe.

You may one day have the luck to dive into this remote and golden wilderness yourself. But even if you enjoy it only through films and beautiful photographs, the need to protect the kelp forest's future remains urgent. Think of it as environmental insurance. As a valuable economic resource. And as a legacy for our children, and the children of the sea otter, and the glowing garibaldi, and the squid.

Kelp forest secrets

- The lively garibaldi, an orangy-red fish brighter than a Halloween pumpkin, enjoys state protection. It is California's official marine fish.

- Ice cream, salad dressing, even your toothpaste contain algin, a thickener from the useful kelp plant.

- Instead of roots, a kelp "tree" grabs onto rocky reefs with a holdfast. This gnarly mass looks like colorful fingers. Or fat spaghetti!

- *Macrocystis*, the giant kelp, is the speediest grower and tallest plant in the sea. In 24 hours, it may shoot up two feet. Its only competition on land? Bamboo, which can grow two to three feet each day.

- The purple urchin: prickly enemy number one in Pacific coast kelp forests. This climber has a huge appetite for kelp. It even chomps tough holdfasts, setting the tall "trees" of the forest adrift.

- Some kelp forest residents have lots of candles on their birthday cakes. Garibaldi fishes may reach 18 years, but certain anemone species live a century or more!

- Nudibranchs or sea slugs look like Christmas-tree ornaments against the golden-green of the kelp forest. These tiny meat-eaters arm themselves with the poison harpoons of the prey they bring down.

- A husky sea slug called the navanax follows slime trails to its prey. It can gulp down sea slugs twice its size.

- Bat rays prowl the sandy plains next to the kelp forest for their dinners. To find crabs in hiding, bat rays blow aside the sand with jets of water.

- The kelp forest canopy acts as a waterbed and playpen for playful marine mammals like the seal, the sea otter, and the sea lion.

◀ A tiny nudibranch called the Spanish shawl roams among strawberry anemones. The crayon-bright colors of both species warn other creatures: "We are poisonous—beware!"

Glossary

Algae. Simple plants, living mostly in water, with no true roots, stems, or leaves. Algae includes tiny species and huge plants like the giant kelp.

Algin. A substance found in the cell walls of giant kelp. Algin is often used in food processing to thicken liquid mixtures and make them smoother.

By-catch. Also called incidental kill, this refers to the killing of marine animals through the wasteful, harmful practice of trapping, then throwing away unwanted fish and shellfish from gill nets and other capture methods used by the fishing industry.

Bryozoans. Often called moss animals, these small lacy creatures live in colonies. Some species find homes on kelp blades.

Canopy. The upper layer of foliage in a kelp forest, branching across the surface of the sea. On land, the top story of a rainforest is also called a canopy.

Chromatophore. Specialized pigment cells found in the skin that cause rapid changes in color and texture. Some species of fish and the octopus have many chromatophores.

Cryptic coloration. Camouflage worn by a kelp forest animal to hide from predators or disguise themselves in order to ambush prey.

Drift kelp. As they age, the fronds of kelp drop like leaves. The dead matter is called drift kelp and it's eaten by scores of creatures.

El Nino events. Periodic cycles of warming in the world's oceans. Although El Nino events occur naturally, they appear to be getting more extreme and frequent, likely due to global warming.

Filter feeder. An animal that gets its nutrition by filtering food particles from the sea or waters around it.

Frond and blade. Frond is the part of the kelp resembling the branch or vine of a plant growing on land. The broad, flat blades of kelp are similar to leaves on a land plant.

Haptera. Finger-like fibers that make up the holdfast and glue it to the rock.

Holdfast. A tangled mass of tough strands or haptera that firmly anchor the kelp plant to a rocky reef or other hard surface on the ocean floor. Giant kelp and other algae species use holdfasts instead of roots.

Hydroids. Small animals, related to corals and living in colonies under the sea. They often grow in tree-like shapes. Hydrozoan "branches" are covered with rows of tiny polyps that catch bits of plankton food drifting by.

Isopods. Small flat animals that eat vegetable matter. They are very numerous and look similar to shrimp.

Kelp highway. Name given to the nearly continuous stands of kelp forest that once ran from Japan across the northern Pacific to North America and into South America.

Nematocysts. Stinging cells, like tiny harpoons, possessed by numerous hunters in the kelp forest. They are often found in the tentacles of anemones, gorgonian corals, and jellyfish.

Plankton. The rich living "soup" of the sea, made of free-floating plant matter like algae and diatoms, and animal matter like larvae, krill, and copepods. Plankton washes through the kelp forest constantly and nourishes the entire web of life in the sea.

Pneumatocyst. The floats or bladders of bull kelp and *Macrocystis* or giant kelp. They are filled with gas. They hold up the heavy fronds of the plant, giving it buoyancy and helping the kelp grow towards the sunlight.

Sloughing. In the same way that dead leaves fall from a tree, kelp plants shed blades and fronds as they age. This process is called sloughing (rhymes with 'roughing.') The dead matter, called drift kelp, becomes food for countless creatures. Sloughing also makes room for new growth.

Stipes. The main stalk or stem of a giant kelp or bull kelp plant. Stipes are long hollow tubes, their cell walls made stiffer with a substance called algin.

Surge. The action of ocean waves underwater, as they move through the kelp forest. Storms above the ocean create huge surges below the surface, at times as strong as mini-hurricanes.

About the author & photographers

During his career, Howard Hall has become one of the world's most respected underwater filmmakers and animal behavioralists. He's received six Emmys, a Golden Panda, and numerous other honors for his "blue chip" natural history films. A multi-talented man whose energy matches his high-speed subject matter, Howard did this book as a print companion to "Seasons in the Sea" and "Forest in the Sea," his kelp forest films for PBS television.

Ably assisted by his wife Michele, an underwater photographer and award-winning film producer herself, Howard has created a spectacular, much-praised series of films in IMAX format, including "Deep Sea 3D" in 2006.

Michele's photos appear on pp 4-5; 6 bottom; 19; 26; and 47 left. Mark Conlin contributed the photos on page 7 and 12-13. All other photos are by Howard Hall.

Special thanks

- Diana Barnhart, Education and Marine Science Advisor
- Dr. Richard Murphy of the Ocean Futures Society
- Dr. Jack Engle, Director of Research at Tatman Foundation and the Channel Islands Research Program
- Ron McPeak and Dale Glantz of Kelco Corporation, part of Monsanto Kelco Alginates/ISP Inc.
- Photographers Mark Conlin, Bob Cranston and Norbert Wu

Diving the kelp forests

Kelp forests occur globally off portions of North America, South America, Australia, New Zealand, South Africa, the Antarctic peninsula, and around certain islands. The once-fabulous kelp forests off the California coast have shrunk considerably. Popular dive spots do remain in the Channel Island National Marine Sanctuary; off the coast within the Monterey Bay National Marine Sanctuary; parts of Puget Sound and Barkley Sound, Washington; and Baja California as far south as San Ignacio Lagoon.

Live kelp forests for non-divers

- Monterey Bay Aquarium's huge, 28-foot-high kelp forest display, where numerous marine species interact and are fed twice daily by divers. Engrossing hands-on kelp lab for kids. (www.mbayaq.org)
- Birch Aquarium, Scripps Institution of Oceanography, La Jolla in San Diego County. Admire the kelp forest ecosystem in their 70,000-gallon tank. Their thoughtful film, "Ghost Forest," shows the clear impact of human activity on kelp forests and critters from abalone to fish species. (www.aquarium.ucsd.edu)
- Two Oceans Aquarium in Cape Town, South Africa. A huge kelp forest display in 20-foot-high tanks includes key species: rockhopper penguins, schools of pilchard, and galjoen, the national fish of South Africa. Twice daily feedings. (www.aquarium.co.za)

Good websites & helping organizations

- Monterey Bay Aquarium, 886 Cannery Row, Monterey CA 93950. Entertaining, useful website, with downloadable "Kelp Forest" poster and a "kelp cam" that lets you check out the 3-story, 343,000-gallon kelp forest exhibit online, where sharks patrol and divers feed hungry species. (www.mbayaq.org)
- The Halls' own website combines stirring photos and amazing video clips with stories of their underwater adventures, interviews, and amusing tales of "kelp moles" and other surprises. (www.howardhall.com)

- Oceanlink, an excellent interactive site where kids around the globe can "Ask a Scientist" and get answers from experts. Their "All about the Ocean" section is worth checking out. (www.oceanlink.island/net/ask)
- Inch in a pinch. An informative, kid-friendly website where a fishy character named "gutsy garibaldi" leads kids and teachers on a grand tour of the kelp forest. (www.inchinapinch.com)
- Educator special: A nice roundup, including photos, of kelp forests and their ecosystems worldwide. Scientific but clear language, excellent diagrams that contrast and compare kelp forests by type. (www.life.bio.sunysb.edu/marinebio/kelpforest)
- Earthwatch Institute, 3 Clock Tower Place, #100, Maynard MA 01754. This global organization gets results by linking scientists, teams of volunteers, and research projects on nearshore habitats, invertebrates, coastal ecology, and more. Some teams accept kids ten and up. Teachers, students: check for scholarships, curriculum materials, and "Live from the Field" opportunities. (www.earthwatch.org)
- Part of the larger national system, the Monterey Bay National Marine Sanctuary protects 276 miles of California coastline and over 5,300 square miles of ocean, including the kelp forests near shore. MBNMS has interpretive centers, sponsors Ocean Fairs and community education programs. The complex website includes more info on kelp forests and links to other sanctuaries, such as the Channel Islands and Olympic Coast NMS. (www.oceanservice.noaa.gov)

To learn more

Books

- *The Amber Forest* by Ronald McPeak, Dale Glantz, and Carole Shaw. (Watersport Publishing 1988). Far from new but still invaluable: timeless information, hundreds of superb photos and creature closeups.
- *Life in a Kelp Forest* by Mary Jo Rhodes & David Hall. (Scholastic/Children's Press 2005). Very good visuals and text for younger readers in 48 pages.
- *Kelp Forests* by Judith Conner & Charles Baxter. (Monterey Bay Aquarium Publishing 1989). Another oldie but goodie crammed with detailed data, especially on kelp varieties.
- *California Marine Life* by Marty Snyderman. (Roberts Rinehart Publishing 1998). A grand field guide, key for kelp forest, tidepool, and nearshore identifications.
- You may also want to read *A Frenzy of Sharks* and *A Charm of Dolphins*, the Halls' other two nature books for the Jean-Michel Cousteau Presents series.

Videos & DVDs

- "Forest in the Sea." ABC Video, 1991. VHS. 25 minutes. Produced and filmed by Howard Hall. Extraordinary footage of lobster molting, wolf eel scarfing up helpless lobster, kelp fishes male and female, and other behavioral sequences.
- "Seasons in the Sea." PBS Nature/BBC special, 1990. VHS. 1 hour. Golden Panda award-winning kelp forest film by Howard Hall.
- "Secrets of the Ocean Realm." PBS, 1997. VHS. 5-part series, filmed and produced by the Halls. The 30-minute segment "Cathedral in the Sea" is on kelp forests.

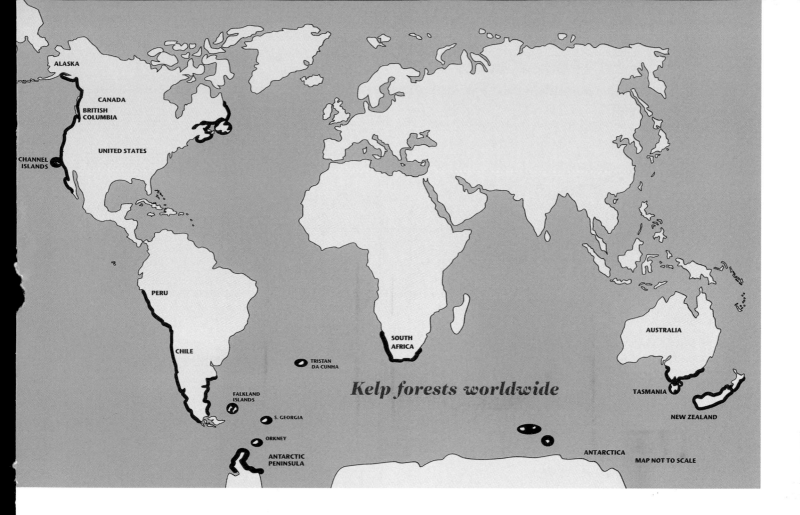

ALASKA

CANADA

BRITISH
COLUMBIA

UNITED STATES

CHANNEL
ISLANDS

PERU

CHILE

TRISTAN
DA CUNHA

SOUTH
AFRICA

Kelp forests worldwide

AUSTRALIA

TASMANIA

NEW ZEALAND

FALKLAND
ISLANDS

S. GEORGIA

ORKNEY

ANTARCTIC
PENINSULA

ANTARCTICA

MAP NOT TO SCALE

◄ A fish called the Irish lord tears into a decorator crab dinner. Both animals live on the rocky reef of a Canadian kelp forest.

►Smaller sea creatures often use larger, more dangerous ones for protection. Tiny jack fish and wee crabs cuddle under the velvety bell of a giant jellyfish. They are protected by mucus coatings on their skin and shells.

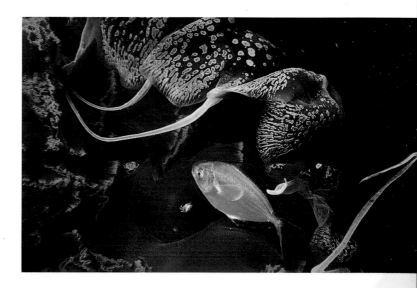

Index

Photographs are numbered in **boldface** and follow the print references after **PP** (photo page).